THE RAF

1918–2018

Julian Hale

Shire Publications, an imprint of Osprey Publishing Ltd
c/o Bloomsbury Publishing Plc
PO Box 883, Oxford, OX1 9PL, UK

Or

c/o Bloomsbury Publishing Inc.
1385 Broadway, 5th Floor, New York, NY 10018, USA

E-mail: shire@bloomsbury.com
www.shirebooks.co.uk

SHIRE is a trademark of Osprey Publishing Ltd, a division of Bloomsbury Publishing Plc.

First published in Great Britain in 2018.

A CIP catalogue record for this book is available from the British Library.

Shire Library no. 844.

ISBN: PB: 978 1 78442 243 1

         ePub: 978 1 78442 244 8

         ePDF: 978 1 78442 245 5

         XML: 978 1 78442 246 2

18 19 20 21 22   10 9 8 7 6 5 4 3 2 1

Typeset in Garamond Pro and Gill Sans

Page layouts by PDQ Digital Media Solutions, Bungay, UK

Printed and bound in India by Replika Press Private Ltd.

Shire Publications supports the Woodland Trust, the UK's leading woodland conservation charity. Between 2014 and 2018 our donations are being spent on their Centenary Woods project in the UK.

COVER IMAGE
Spitfires N3200 (foreground) and P9374 (background) were Mark I Spitfires lost in Northern France in 1940. Both have been restored to flying condition and can be seen at the Imperial War Museum, Duxford. (Courtesy of John Dibbs)

TITLE PAGE IMAGE
The English Electric Canberra entered service as a fast, unarmed bomber to replace the Mosquito and went on to fulfil a variety of tasks. B.6 bombers are pictured in 1954.

CONTENTS PAGE IMAGE
An RAF Boeing Chinnook crewman observed that it is 'the armour plated workhorse of the battlefield, a bus that handles like a sports car.' The aircraft has seen action as a heavy lift helicopter from the Falklands to Afghanistan.

ACKNOWLEDGEMENTS
Images are acknowledged as follows:

Page 3, Crown copyright 2007; page 50, Crown copyright 2016; page 55, Crown copyright 2007; page 56, Crown copyright 2014; page 57, Crown copyright 2012; page 57, Crown copyright 2015; page 58, Crown copyright 2014; page 59, Crown copyright 2010; page 60 (Top), Crown copyright 2008; page 60 (bottom), Crown copyright 2014.

All remaining images courtesy of the Royal Air Force Museum.

CONTENTS

INTRODUCTION

THE ROYAL AIR FORCE HAS played a role in almost every campaign undertaken by the United Kingdom since 1918. Looming large is the Second World War, when the RAF contained over a million personnel and played a key role in delivering final victory. Aerial operations continue in 2018 in the Middle East, an area familiar to the RAF of the 1920s and 1930s, while the renewed threat from Russia in the twenty-first century recalls the tensions of the Cold War.

Although the structure and size of the RAF have changed, the strong foundations laid in the early years means that much of the service remains recognisable today, and the vision of Marshal of the Royal Air Force Lord Trenchard, the 'father of the RAF', of a small, highly professional cadre, remains as true now as it did at the beginning. The influence of the world's oldest air force can be seen in the technical, organisational and cultural bonds formed over many years between the RAF and Commonwealth and allied air forces.

This book is intended to be a short introduction to the RAF. Many important aspects of the air force, its organisation and its history have received only cursory mention. For those who wish to explore further, there are a vast number of books and articles covering almost every facet of the RAF's history, a few of which are listed at the end of this book. It is hoped that this slim volume may whet the reader's appetite to learn more.

OPPOSITE:
Marshal of the
Royal Air Force
Lord Trenchard,
the 'father of
the RAF'.

FORMATION (1911–19)

IN THE EARLY years of the twentieth century, the world's major powers began to recognise the potential military value of balloons, airships and, in particular, aeroplanes. Great Britain was no exception and in 1911, the Air Battalion of the Royal Engineers was formed. Around the same time, the Royal Navy established a flying school at Eastchurch on the Isle of Sheppey.

In an attempt to coordinate the aerial interests of the two services, the Royal Flying Corps (RFC), consisting of a Military Wing, a Naval Wing and a Central Flying School (CFS), was formed in April 1912. However, with only a consultative sub-committee as an inter-service authority, there was little coordination between the Military and Naval Wings. This was underlined in July 1914, when the Naval Wing separated from the RFC and the Royal Naval Air Service (RNAS) was formed.

At the outbreak of the First World War, the RFC sent most of its aircraft to France with the British Expeditionary Force, and during the next three and a half years supported the army in a variety of tasks. The RNAS operated against German U-boats and airships, formed a number of squadrons to serve on the Western Front and assumed partial responsibility for Home Defence duties.

Although the RFC and RNAS eventually succeeded in defeating the German airship raids in the autumn of 1916, a much more potent threat emerged the following year when,

South African soldier and statesman Jan Smuts, author of a report from which emerged the Royal Air Force.

on 7 July 1917, a formation of Gotha aeroplanes attacked London in daylight. Although casualties among the civilian population were fairly light, the feeble response by the defences caused outrage. The Chief of the Imperial General Staff, Sir William Robertson, revealed in a letter that during a cabinet meeting on the day of the Gotha raid, panic was not confined to the population at large: 'one would have thought the whole world was coming to an end…I could not get a word in edgeways.'

In response, the government commissioned a report into the state of home defences. Two reports were written by Lieutenant-General Jan Smuts, the famous Boer soldier and South Africa's representative in the Imperial War Cabinet. The first sensibly recommended a single, unified command to control all the fighter squadrons, anti-aircraft batteries, searchlights and observation posts throughout the UK.

In the second report, Smuts came to three conclusions: that aircraft were of strategic importance; that the Germans realised this; and that the UK's aircraft industry was capable of supporting a strategic air offensive against Germany. Significantly, Smuts wrote of aircraft:

> As far as can at present be foreseen there is absolutely no limit to the scale of its future independent war use. And the day may not be far off when aerial operations with their devastation of enemy lands and destruction of industrial and populous centres on a vast scale may become the principal operations of war, to which the older forms of military and naval operations may become secondary and subordinate…

Smuts went on to suggest that an Air Ministry should be established to coordinate planning and industrial resources

Sopwith 2F.1 Camels aboard HMS *Furious* for the raid on the German airship base at Tondern in July 1918. The Camels destroyed two Zeppelins in the world's first carrier airstrike.

and administer the new air force, which would be created from an amalgamation of the RFC and RNAS. In addition, a fleet of bombers was to be created with the specific task of attacking German industrial towns.

Although there was opposition to an independent air force, notably from the RFC's commander, Hugh Trenchard, who argued that an air force should be created after the war had ended, the government pressed ahead. On 20 November 1917, a bill to constitute an Air Ministry received Royal Assent as 'The Air Force Act'. The merger of the RFC and RNAS officially took place on 1 April 1918, creating the Royal Air Force (RAF).

The creation of a new service did not have a great impact on the men in action around the world. During the final months of the First World War, the RAF fought with the army in a series of offensives, while British bombers attacked German industrial centres in a sporadic fashion and with somewhat limited success. More positively, in July 1918, the RAF carried out the world's first carrier-borne strike, when a few Sopwith Camels took off from HMS *Furious* to attack the Zeppelin base at Tondern in northern Germany.

By the end of the First World War, the RAF had become the largest air force in the world, performing a wide variety of roles and making a valuable contribution to the victories of 1918.

A SILVER AIR FORCE (1919–39)

AFTER THE EUPHORIA following the First World War had ended, it was time for sober assessments to be made. Of immediate importance was the rapid but necessary scaling down of the three services, and the RAF was no exception. There was even some doubt over the continued viability of an independent air service. Winston Churchill, the new Secretary of State for Air, asked Trenchard, now Chief of the Air Staff, to give his views on the future size and shape of the air force; a White Paper was duly published in 1919, setting out Trenchard's views. In this, he emphasised strict economy, the value of training to form a small but elite cadre and the role of the RAF bomber force as a (future) deterrent. To complement this separate identity, a new uniform was designed, different medals were authorised and a revised system of organisation and ranks was adopted. Other details, such as an RAF March Past and the creation of squadron badges by the College of Arms, came into being in the following years.

The attacks upon the RAF by the two older services became part of the air force's founding legend, in which there is a degree of truth. One civil servant, Sir Maurice Dean, wrote that 'they considered it an upstart and its officers for the most part socially impossible… [The RAF] was an innovation and the way of innovators in Britain is hard. The first instinct is to ignore, the second is to despise, the third is to attack', adding that he saw the RAF 'as the beleaguered maiden, the army and navy as the dragon and its mate, and Trenchard as

OPPOSITE:
Gloster Gladiators tied together in formation, 1938. The last biplane fighter in RAF service, the Gladiator flew in a number of theatres during the early years of the Second World War.

It is ill-remembered that the RAF controlled the Royal Navy's Fleet Air Arm during the inter-war period. Here, Fairey IIIFs fly in formation over HMS *Eagle*.

St George'. Several serious but unsuccessful political attempts were made to destroy the independence of the RAF during the 1920s. The matter rested until 1937, when a committee chaired by Sir Thomas Inskip decided that the Royal Navy should control its own air service. Nevertheless, it was another two years before the navy formally took over control of its own air service, and it would begin the Second World War with a force of largely obsolescent aircraft.

Meanwhile, Britain's considerably expanded empire required constant attention, and this provided the RAF with a *raison d'être* during a time of financial austerity. Indeed, reconnaissance, leaflet-dropping and the bombing of hostile areas became the most important roles of the air force in the inter-war period.

The RAF would prove its value as an inexpensive alternative to the army in 1920, when it successfully countered an uprising by Mohammed bin Abdullah (known as 'The Mad Mullah') in British Somaliland. The army's proposal for two infantry divisions and the construction of a permanent railway was obviously expensive and, at a time of financial stringency,

very unwelcome. A few obsolete Airco D.H.9s were sent and, in early 1920, began to attack Abdullah's main camp. His army soon began to retreat and Abdullah was forced to flee to Abyssinia, where he was killed the following year. Later, the Colonial Secretary, Leo Amery, wrote that 'All was over in three weeks…at £77,000, [it was] the cheapest war in history.'

Further validation was not long in coming. As the cost of garrisoning Mesopotamia (known from 1922 as Iraq) was becoming prohibitive, Churchill asked Trenchard if he would be 'prepared to take Mesopotamia on' and offered the RAF another £5–£7 million to do so. In 1922 the RAF took over the region's garrison and raised a number of armoured car companies. From an early stage, the RAF was heavily involved in quelling insurgency by the Kurds in the north of the country, as well as halting attempts by Turkey to re-establish its control of the region. In the years following, uprisings by Sheikh Mahmud, one-time governor of a region of Iraq, were frustrated by operations which continued sporadically until 1931.

The mandate of Palestine witnessed only occasional unrest until the mid-1930s, when antagonism between Jews and

The RAF formed its own armoured car units to serve in Palestine, Transjordan and Iraq during the inter-war period. A Fairey Gordon overflies a unit near the Jordan valley in 1936.

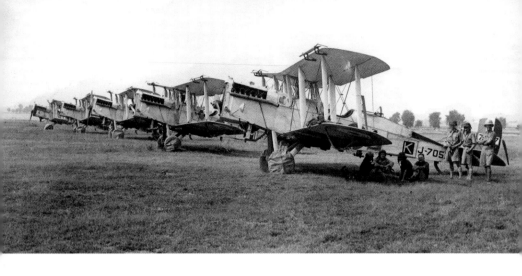

De Havilland D.H.9As at Risalpur, India. The Liberty-powered 'Ninak' became the quintessential aircraft of aerial policing in the 1920s, serving successfully in India and Mesopotamia.

Arabs began to seriously threaten peace in the country. After attempts to police the area by air alone failed, control was passed to the army and until 1939 the two services worked together to try to remedy the situation. However, the Second World War would only postpone further troubles in the region for another six years or so.

The North-West Frontier of India was rarely quiet, and in 1925, when serious incursions began against army outposts in the region, air operations were the chosen method of striking back. The commander of the operation was Wing Commander R.C.M. Pink and the campaign became known as 'Pink's War'. After dropping warning leaflets for a week proved fruitless, bombing began over a two-month period, after which the rebels called for peace. A rebellion which occurred against the Western-influenced King Amanullah in Afghanistan in 1928 became widespread and it was not long before the capital, Kabul, was threatened. On 23 December, the first RAF airlift of British nationals began from Kabul. With the co-operation of the rebel leader, further flights were made, often in freezing conditions, through to February 1929, including the evacuation of the abdicated king, his brother and the latter's harem. Further minor actions followed over the years and aerial activity of one form or another on the frontier was more or less constant.

Life for RAF personnel around the empire was often wearisome and heat was a major source of discomfort, with temperatures in Iraq sometimes reaching 52°C, while sickness from tropical diseases was widespread. Flight Lieutenant J.M. Cohu, who joined 27 Squadron in India in 1934, remembered:

The weather was normally excellent for flying and the principal hazards were the possibility of engine failure and of rifle-fire over tribal territory. There was also the constant danger of collision with the large hawks which pestered the air approaches and caused at least one fatal flying accident in my time. Ransom notes were always carried in case of forced landing…in the hot season…work started at dawn and finished at about one pm when the temperature was near the hundred mark. Sleep at night under mosquito nets was often difficult, and sometimes a hellish wind off the desert sent the temperature as high as 115-degrees F. The women and children fled early in the season to the hill stations…The men followed later, each for a few weeks in turn, and as there were so few of the one sex and so many of the other the scandals were frequent…The season of the year made little difference to the upper air temperature… and the cold was intense in the unheated open cockpits. However, on the run to the north-east one had at least the privilege of a unique view of part of the highest mountain range in the world…The frontier at this time was relatively peaceful – though the term 'peaceful' could never be truly descriptive of the Frontier Province – and the sound and sight of our aircraft over tribal territory was usually sufficient deterrent to potential law-breakers…For the sportsmen [while on leave] there were all kinds of shooting and fishing, from tiger to small game…There was golf at 6,000 feet at Gulmarg…[and in] winter Gulmarg provided super skiing…Life on an RAF squadron on the Frontier in

RAF Halton provided a steady flow of well-trained personnel from the beginning. Halton apprentices work on the Rolls-Royce Kestrel engine of a Hawker Hart Trainer in 1937.

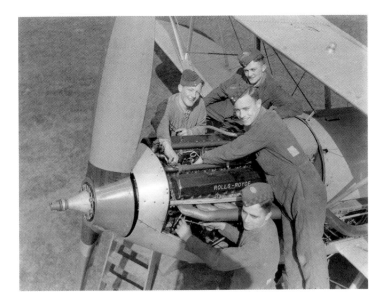

the early thirties was for many a time of hard work and hard play, full of interest and new experiences. Others found it a hardship with separation from their loved ones and for these the days and months were long indeed. Yet for all it was an unforgettable experience and a challenge which nearly all rose to meet.

The efficacy and morality of imperial air policing was much discussed at the time and in the years since. The relative frugality of RAF operations made them popular with British governments of the 1920s and 1930s. Nevertheless, a small but vociferous minority of MPs continued to protest at the morality of bombing civilians and one senior RAF officer in Iraq resigned his post in protest. One historian has written that 'had there been a wider public awareness of the often harsh effects of air policing, it might not have continued for as long as it did.' Trenchard himself wrote that 'when punishment is intended, the punishment must be severe, continuous, and even prolonged.'

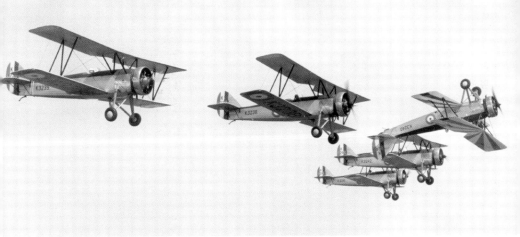

Avro Tutors of the Central Flying School practise aerobatics in 1933.

Trenchard had stressed the importance of training and building an experienced cadre of personnel, upon which the RAF could expand in time of war. To facilitate this, three main institutions were established. In the first place, the new service lacked a college similar to those which served the army and navy. Trenchard saw that this needed to be quickly rectified and in 1920 the RAF College Cranwell was founded, with the famous Hall being opened in 1934, although it is interesting to note that some temporary accommodation dating from the First World War survived until as late as 1953. The RAF College, irreverently known as 'Sleaford Tech', and the nearby airfield continue to be used to this day. In 1922, a Staff College to provide on-going tuition for officers was opened at Andover.

The second institution was a school for apprentices, where those joining the service as airmen would learn to maintain the air force's increasingly complex aircraft; a new camp for RAF apprentices was duly opened at Halton in 1922.

Robert Smith-Barry revolutionised the training syllabus during the First World War by teaching pupils to deal with dangerous manoeuvres in a controlled manner. In 1920, the Central Flying School assumed the role of training future flying instructors and, by embodying the practices laid down by Smith-Barry, ensured that the same high standards were upheld throughout the service.

A Supermarine S.6b during the 1931 Schneider Trophy competition. The 2,300hp S.6b was the ultimate version of R.J. Mitchell's seaplanes and later set a World Speed Record of 407.5mph.

These institutions completed the basic training structure for the RAF. However, it was obvious that a reserve of ready-trained personnel would be needed if and when the time came to expand the air force. Thus it was that in 1924, after some political debate, permission to form a small Auxiliary Air Force (later the Royal Auxiliary Air Force or RAuxAF) was given. RAuxAF squadrons were made from a core of regular RAF personnel, supported by reservists, who made up the remainder. Although sometimes looked at askance by the regular squadrons, the auxiliaries acquitted themselves well when war came in 1939. Despite numerous organisational changes over the years and a move away from the provision of aircrew, the RAuxAF continues to provide a reserve of trained personnel for the RAF.

Another method of attracting entrants was through the University Air Squadrons, the first two of which (Oxford and Cambridge) were formed in 1925. For their members, they presented a reasonably affordable introduction to

The 'Chain Home' radar station at Poling, West Sussex. The radar network on the east coast of the UK was an integral part of the 'Dowding System' during the Battle of Britain.

flying and many former UAS members would serve with distinction in the Second World War. The fifteen University Air Squadrons, administered from Cranwell, continue to train future RAF aircrew.

Another important step which provided further personnel was the formation in 1936 of the Royal Air Force Volunteer Reserve (RAFVR), a 'citizen air force', in which all those who qualified started with the rank of sergeant and received flying training for free. In the twenty-first century, the RAFVR provides instructors for the Air Cadet Organisation and the University Air Squadrons.

During the Second World War, these reserve organisations provided the air force with a valuable pool of airmen, especially important in the critical early months of the war. A large-scale structural reorganisation of the RAF was initiated in the late 1930s and several Commands, the most prominent being Fighter, Bomber and Coastal Commands, were formed in 1936.

For much of the public during the 1920s and 1930s, it was the air displays that epitomised the RAF. The Hendon

Known as 'Stuffy' for his quiet demeanour, Air Chief Marshal Dowding played a key role in preparing and leading Fighter Command in the Battle of Britain.

air displays dazzled spectators with demonstrations of the RAF's prowess, ranging from simulated bombing operations on mock targets to formation air displays given by fighter squadrons flying elegant aluminium-doped biplanes.

More serious were the numerous world record-setting altitude and distance flights made by RAF aircraft during the inter-war period, as well as participation in the Schneider Trophy seaplane races. Eschewing the flying boats previously fielded in the early 1920s, which were rendered obsolete by the fast monoplanes of other nations, Supermarine, Rolls-Royce and the Air Ministry collaborated on a series of powerful and streamlined seaplanes, which proved victorious in 1927, 1929 and 1931, winning the trophy outright. Most important, however, was the valuable work done by Supermarine and Rolls-Royce on advanced aircraft and engine design, which was to prove invaluable when the new generation of aircraft was designed in the late 1930s.

The UK's poor financial position after the First World War forced cuts to the armed services, and in 1919, at the request of the Treasury, the 'Ten Year Rule' was instigated, in which it was decided that no major war would be fought for at least ten years and therefore no increase in defence expenditure was necessary. However, this 'rule' was carried forward until 1932 when, almost too late, it was finally abandoned.

During 1933 and 1934, it became clear that Germany, under Adolf Hitler, was rearming. The idea of the RAF providing a 'bomber deterrent' was a guiding principle in the post-1918 years; as early as 1916, Trenchard had written that 'the aeroplane is not a defence against the aeroplane…' The idea that, in Prime Minister Stanley Baldwin's words, 'the bomber will always get through', was so strong that it took some effort to force the belief that an adequate fighter presence for the UK was necessary. The main result of this about-turn was a series of eight Expansion Schemes which quickly succeeded one another from 1934 to 1939. Although they failed in their aim to prevent German aggression, by demonstrating that the UK was prepared to match them 'keel for keel', they did provide the RAF with aircraft and equipment which was (just) adequate when war started in 1939. Many light bombers, relatively easy to produce and presumed to be sufficient to support an expeditionary force on the continent, were built as a show of force or 'window dressing'. These included the Hawker series of biplanes and the more modern Fairey Battle and Bristol Blenheim. Better designs were ordered later, notably the Vickers Wellington, which entered service before the war, and the specifications which eventually produced the four-engined Short Stirling, Handley Page Halifax and Avro Lancaster were issued.

Perhaps the greatest achievement of the Expansion Schemes was to give the RAF a viable force of fighters. Both the Hawker Hurricane and the more advanced Supermarine Spitfire were fast, well-armed monoplane designs and represented a considerable advance in terms of previous designs. Equally important was the remarkably efficient creation of a fighter control system. The invention and development of radar in the late 1930s enabled the accurate reporting of enemy formations approaching the UK coast; the 'Dowding System', named after its chief sponsor and head of Fighter Command, Sir Hugh Dowding, sifted, collated and interpreted this information. All this was just operational in time for the outbreak of the Second World War in September 1939.

TO WAR (1939–45)

I N SEPTEMBER 1939, Germany invaded Poland. The speed of the German advance meant that Britain and France had no time to show any real initiative before Poland surrendered. Shortly after the outbreak of war, several squadrons of Fairey Battles and Hawker Hurricanes accompanied the British Expeditionary Force to France, in the expectation of a campaign in the summer of 1940. The winter and spring of 1939–40 passed with no major action and became known to the press as the 'Phoney War'.

An attempt in the spring to thwart German designs on Scandinavia by landing an Anglo-French force in Norway went badly awry. Pre-empted by a German offensive, the campaign, marked by indecision, ineptitude and confusion, proved a disaster. The RAF tried to provide a measure of air cover with a small force of Hurricanes and obsolete Gloster Gladiators but these, with the Allied troops, were evacuated during May and June.

The campaign in Norway was not over before the German offensive opened in France, Belgium and the Netherlands. The Allied forces were unable to stop the German advance – in one instance, an attempt by Battles and Blenheims to bomb the bridges over the River Meuse at Sedan on 14 May 1940 ended in disaster when forty attackers out of seventy-one were lost. Viewing the continuing attrition of his Hurricane squadrons in France with alarm, Air Chief Marshal Dowding wrote to the Air Ministry on 16 May, advising that:

OPPOSITE: An Avro Lancaster silhouetted over Hamburg during the night of 30/31 January 1943. The bombing of Germany has attracted controversy in the years following the Second World War.

Fairey Battles escorted by French *Armée de l'Air* Curtiss Hawks. The Fairey Battle fell far short of expectations as a light bomber and high losses were sustained during 1940.

…not one fighter will be sent across the Channel however urgent and insistent the appeals for help may be…if the Home Defence Force is drained away in desperate attempts to remedy the situation in France, defeat in France will involve the final, complete and irremediable defeat of this country.

By 26 May, Allied troops were being evacuated from France. The Luftwaffe made repeated attempts to destroy the enclave around Dunkirk and although Fighter Command made determined efforts to intervene, many returning soldiers naturally but mistakenly blamed the RAF for their plight.

With the fall of France, Hitler ordered preparations to begin for a cross-Channel invasion and gave the Luftwaffe the task of establishing air superiority as a preliminary move. Early German attacks on Channel shipping during July and August were sporadic and ill-focused but proved to be a steady drain on the aircraft and pilots of Fighter Command. These were followed by a concentrated series of attacks against British radar stations and airfields. Hundreds of sorties were flown each day and by the beginning of September, the strain was beginning to show on both sides.

Nevertheless, although hard-pressed, Fighter Command held its own. The early warning provided by radar and the

Women's Auxiliary Air Force (WAAF) plotters work at Fighter Command HQ during the Battle of Britain. In 1939, the WAAF was formed to replace male personnel with women where necessary.

efficient communications network usually gave British fighters enough time to be scrambled, and the Luftwaffe's *Experten* found that the Hurricane and Spitfire were not as easy to destroy as previous aircraft they had encountered. Furthermore, Air Vice-Marshal Keith Park, leading Fighter Command's 11 Group, only used his aircraft in small numbers, denying the Germans a 'target-rich' environment. The Luftwaffe not only chronically under-estimated RAF strength during the battle but also mistakenly attacked some airfields in the belief that they were fighter bases. Those radar stations and grass airfields which were bombed were often rapidly made operational again. Furthermore, in late August and early September, the Luftwaffe's attacks lost focus and raids were made on ports and factories, which were not vital to Fighter Command's short-term survival.

In his book *The Last Enemy*, Richard Hillary recounted a typical combat, in which he claimed his first 'kill':

We ran into them at 18,000 feet, twenty yellow-nosed Messerschmitt 109s, about 500 feet above us. Our Squadron strength was eight, and as they came down on

A Hawker Hurricane with pilots of 303 (Polish) Squadron. The Hurricane played a crucial role in the Battle of Britain, while personnel from occupied countries and the empire made a significant contribution to the RAF during the Second World War.

us we went into line astern and turned head on to them…I saw Brian let go a burst of fire at the leading plane, saw the pilot put his machine into a half-roll, and knew that he was mine. Automatically, I kicked the rudder to the left to get him at right angles, turned the gunbutton to 'Fire', and let go in a four-second burst with full deflection. He came right through my sights and I saw the tracer from all eight guns thud home. For a second he seemed to hang motionless; then a jet of red flame shot upwards and he spun out of sight…It had happened.

In September, the Luftwaffe began attacking London by day and night, concentrating on the docklands area. Two large raids on 15 September, later known as 'Battle of Britain Day', saw violent clashes over London and the south-east, resulting in twenty-nine British losses for around sixty German. Shortly afterwards, Hitler abandoned realistic plans for an invasion.

As part of an attempt to defeat Britain through siege, the Luftwaffe initiated the 'Blitz', with nightly raids against London and other British cities, notably Liverpool, Manchester and Coventry. The Blitz ended in May 1941, during which radar-equipped RAF night-fighters had fought back with increasing success and Luftwaffe units were steadily withdrawn from France in preparation for service in Russia and the Mediterranean.

A decision by Fighter Command to fly aggressive fighter sweeps over Europe from 1941 met with only modest success. Although the RAF claimed 731 German fighters between June and December 1941, actual Luftwaffe losses were only 154, against Fighter Command losses of 411. The sweeps forced the RAF's fighters to fight over enemy territory and the Channel in much the same way as the Luftwaffe had in 1940, and further heavy RAF losses were incurred in support of the Dieppe Raid in August 1942. Compounding the problem was the introduction of the formidable Focke-Wulf Fw190 in 1941, which remained superior or equal to most Allied fighters until the end of the war. However, the Luftwaffe's strength in France waned as pressure in Russia and the Mediterranean mounted, while increasingly bold US daylight attacks on Germany forced a gradual withdrawal of fighter units to defend the Reich.

German attacks on Britain did not stop in 1941. The targeting of medieval German cities by Bomber Command resulted in the 'Baedeker Raids' (named after the popular tourist guidebooks) on historic British towns in 1942. With D-Day approaching during the spring of 1944, a half-hearted and ineffective offensive, known to the Luftwaffe as Operation *Steinbock* and to the British as the 'Baby Blitz', was made on targets in the south of the UK.

From spring 1944, the RAF and USAAF initiated the Allied 'Transportation Plan', a campaign to weaken German forces in preparation for the Normandy invasion, in which

A Hawker Typhoon with pilots of 257 Squadron, 1943. Rugged and heavily armed, the Typhoon made a fine ground-attack aircraft and those of the Second Tactical Air Force were heavily engaged during and after D-Day.

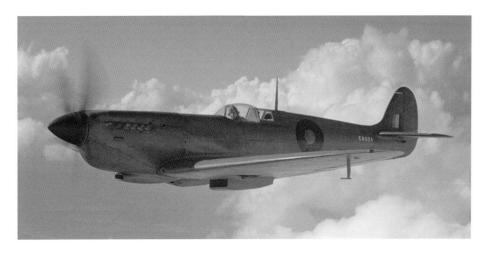

A photo-reconnaissance Supermarine Spitfire PR. XI, 1943. Although chiefly remembered as a fighter, the Spitfire served in many theatres and in a variety of roles for many years.

the primary target was the French transport infrastructure. The most significant RAF contributions to D-Day were the establishment of air superiority over the landing beaches, without which the invasion could not have been launched, and the provision of hundreds of aircraft, towing gliders and carrying parachute troops, to important points behind the German positions in the early hours of 6 June. With the Allied armies securely ashore, the RAF began to establish airfields behind the front-line. Teams of engineers rapidly laid down runways and taxiways, and, as early as 10 June, Allied squadrons began operating from the first temporary airfields. Dozens of airstrips were eventually constructed, allowing essential stores to be flown in, urgent casualties to be flown out and the fighter-bombers of the Second Tactical Air Force to operate in close support of the armies.

The supporting squadrons moved with the Allied armies as they liberated France, Belgium and the Netherlands and the RAF also provided transport and air cover, first for the unsuccessful Arnhem operation in September 1944 and then for the crossing of the Rhine in March 1945. A temporary but not fatal setback occurred when, in a final gamble and at great cost, the Luftwaffe launched Operation *Bodenplatte*, a wide-scale air attack on the Allied airfields, on New Year's Day, 1945.

Soon after D-Day, the first V-1 flying bombs were launched against the UK. These were followed in September by the supersonic V-2 rocket, which was immune to aerial interception. The RAF response was to use fighters to destroy the relatively vulnerable V-1s in the air, either by gunfire or by tipping them over with the fighter's own wing, while the temporary V-2 sites were attacked where they could be found. In 1944, the RAF's first jet-powered squadron became operational, equipped with Gloster Meteors, and these joined in the defence against the V-1s. As the war in Europe came to an end, the transport and bomber squadrons flew humanitarian aid missions to the starving Dutch population during Operation *Manna*, before repatriating thousands of Allied prisoners of war from Europe to the UK.

The Central Interpretation Unit, staffed by personnel from all walks of life, made a number of important intelligence breakthroughs. Constance Babington Smith, one of the most skilled Photographic Interpreters, is pictured studying a photograph.

Bomber Command's first forays against Germany were mainly armed-reconnaissance missions against the German fleet. These ended in disaster when, on 18 December 1939, in the 'Battle of the Heligoland Bight', twelve Wellingtons out of a force of twenty-two were lost to German fighters. From this point, Bomber Command was forced to operate by night, dropping leaflets and attacking German cities in small numbers, a situation which prevailed until 1942.

While nocturnal operations led to fewer casualties, navigation problems meant that crews had great difficulty in locating targets. The Butt Report of October 1941 showed that of those aircraft recorded as attacking their target, only one in three got within five miles. Over the important targets

Although the best RAF bomber at the outbreak of the Second World War, the Vickers Wellington suffered heavily against German day fighters. It later provided good service as a night-bomber until 1943.

of the Ruhr, where frequent cloud combined with industrial haze to make target-finding very difficult, only *one in ten* aircraft got within five miles. As Bomber Command provided the only means of striking directly at Germany, solutions had to be found and they came in the form of technology. Among these were Gee, a navigational aid introduced in 1942; Oboe, a highly accurate bombing aid introduced the same year; and H2S, a ground-mapping radar introduced in 1943. Tactics also improved: bombers were concentrated into a single stream to swamp the German defences, a Pathfinder Force was created in 1942 to mark targets accurately, and incendiary bombs were found to be more destructive than high explosive ones. Four-engined bombers, capable of carrying heavier bomb-loads over greater distances, were introduced: the Stirling and Halifax in 1941 and the Lancaster, the future backbone of Bomber Command, in 1942. Sir Arthur Harris, appointed as head of

Sir Archibald Sinclair (left) and Air Chief Marshal Portal were Minister of Air and Chief of the Air Staff respectively. They led the RAF through most of the Second World War.

Bomber Command in 1942, promised to put these changes to the test when he declared: 'They sowed the wind and now they are going to reap the whirlwind.'

Although German cities could now be found, accurate bombing was still very difficult, with a host of factors, including weather conditions, the location of the target, enemy defences and chance all playing a role. Thus, a gradual shift to the 'area bombing' method became established, as much by necessity as by choice, and this was codified in the Air Ministry's 1942 Area Bombing Directive. Although the Directive issued after the 1943 Allied Conference in Casablanca provided a list of prioritised industrial targets, Harris concluded that Bomber Command could attack any German city with a population of 100,000 or over.

In 1943, Harris unleashed his command against Germany in a campaign which was to last some twelve months. In the spring, a series of raids was made against the industrial heartland of the Ruhr, followed by the famous 'Dambusters Raid' in May, in which the crews of 617 Squadron destroyed two hydroelectric dams in the Ruhr valley. A short sequence of raids was made against the port of Hamburg, which was devastated by a firestorm in July. With these successes behind him, Harris began a bombing campaign against Berlin itself, stating, 'We can wreck Berlin from end to end if the USAAF come in on it. It will cost between us 400 and 500 aircraft. It will cost Germany the war.' In a succession of raids, during which Harris's crews battled against long distances, poor weather and formidable German defences, Bomber Command lost over one thousand aircraft but did not fatally damage the German capital. Other cities apart from Berlin

Wing Commander Guy Gibson had already completed many missions before he earned the Victoria Cross for leading the 'Dambusters Raid' in 1943. Gibson continued to fly operationally until he was killed in 1944.

were attacked during this difficult period, which culminated in the disastrous Nuremburg Raid of 30/31 March 1944, in which ninety-five aircraft from a force of 795 were lost. By this time, any realistic hope of bringing the war to an early end through bombing was gone, and from April 1944, Bomber Command was tasked with bombing targets in preparation for the invasion of Europe.

Air Marshal Harris (centre) examines a map at Bomber Command HQ. Harris led his command with single-minded determination and was a leading proponent of the 'area-bombing' campaign against Germany.

Although German industrial production rose during 1943 and 1944, it seems certain that Allied bombing prevented it from attaining even greater output. Bomber Command returned to the cities again, including Dresden, in the last months of the war, at a time when the strength of the Third Reich was dwindling amid industrial dispersion, Allied encroachment and administrative chaos.

At the beginning of the war, Coastal Command, tasked with protecting Britain's shipping lanes, found it was hamstrung by obsolete aircraft and equipment. At the centre was the

An Avro Lancaster crew. A standard Bomber Command 'tour' from 1943 was thirty operations. Around 55,000 Bomber Command personnel lost their lives during the strategic bombing offensive.

A De Havilland Mosquito being armed for an anti-shipping strike mission. Although designed as a reconnaissance aircraft using high speed to evade interception, the Mosquito proved successful in a variety of roles.

critically important Battle of the Atlantic; Winston Churchill later wrote that 'the only thing that ever really frightened me during the war was the U-boat peril'. During 1941 and 1942, the Royal Navy and the RAF struggled to contain this threat and merchant shipping losses rose alarmingly. Yet the successful decoding of German communication ciphers, new aircraft and new equipment – allied to fresh tactics and much determination under the successive commands of Air Chief Marshal Sir Philip Joubert de la Ferté and Air Marshal Sir John Slessor – eventually paid dividends.

The most important change for Coastal Command came with the closing of the mid-Atlantic air gap, when American-built Very Long Range Consolidated Liberators were made available in sufficient numbers. Although the U-boats enjoyed further successes in early 1943, the middle of the year saw the threat wane considerably in the face of growing Allied quantitative and qualitative superiority, and from this point, the Battle of the Atlantic was essentially won.

The Mediterranean and North African theatres saw the RAF severely overstretched in the opening phases. The relative weakness of the Italian *Regia Aeronautica* served to mask the fact that Egypt and the strategically important island of Malta were defended by inadequate numbers of obsolescent

The Short Sunderland entered service in 1938 and is chiefly remembered for its part in the Battle of the Atlantic. This aircraft is pictured during the Korean War.

The American-built Very Long Range Consolidated Liberator bridged the mid-Atlantic air gap, previously dominated by the U-boats. The Liberator and many other American aircraft were supplied under the 'Lend-Lease' programme.

aircraft. The arrival of the German *Afrika Korps* in Egypt, and the subsequent series of British reverses, made the need for improved aircraft and tactics obvious. Despite very heavy bombing, Malta was not subdued and the anti-shipping operations launched from the island served to strangle the lifeline to the Axis forces fighting in North Africa. Erwin Rommel wrote: 'With Malta in our hands, the British would have had little chance of exercising any further control over convoy traffic in the Central Mediterranean.'

As more and better equipment began to arrive in Egypt in late 1941 and 1942, so the methods of Arthur Coningham's Desert Air Force in support of the Eighth Army began to improve; these lessons, learned in the heat and dust of North Africa, would pay dividends during the invasion of Europe in 1944. RAF units later participated in the invasions of Sicily and Italy, where progress almost came to a standstill. The

Curtiss Tomahawks of 112 Squadron display the famous 'shark's mouth' insignia. The American Curtiss fighter-bombers were used in great numbers by the RAF in the North African and Mediterranean theatres.

Italian campaign is best remembered for the tragic destruction of the monastery at Monte Cassino, which was bombed in support of Allied troops and which ironically served mainly to impede the advance of the Allied infantry.

Likewise, in the Far East the RAF was completely outclassed when the Japanese invaded Malaya and Burma in December 1941 and the few British aircraft were quickly destroyed. RAF pilot Dennis Davids later wrote that 'in the early stages our aircraft fought well but… our few Hurricanes, P-40s and Buffaloes were no match for the Japanese Air Forces of those days and from the start they were on top'.

One of the greatest challenges for the RAF was maintaining and operating

Air Chief Marshal Tedder commanded RAF forces in the Middle East during the Desert Campaign and in the Mediterranean for the invasion of Italy. He became Air Commander-in-Chief and Deputy Supreme Allied Commander in Europe in 1944.

Indian pilots inspect a waterlogged airfield in Burma. The climate and weather presented a great challenge to operations in the Far East.

aircraft from the primitive airstrips in the Burmese jungle, while the weather and terrain likewise conspired to make navigation and target identification difficult.

Perhaps the greatest contribution made by the RAF in Burma was in the field of supply. In tandem with the USAAF, with which South East Asia Command was formed, large quantities of supplies were ferried across the Himalayas, known as 'the Hump' from India to China. The offensive into Burma in 1943 resulted in an army division being cut off by the Japanese. In its first major resupply operation, the RAF kept the division supplied from the air. When three divisions were surrounded at Kohima later in the year, the operation was repeated.

The Japanese air presence over Burma was swiftly worn down through attrition and resupply problems, and the RAF concentrated a sizeable fighter-bomber force to support the Fourteenth Army from 1943. In 1944, Keith Park arrived to take command of the British air forces in Burma, by which time Allied superiority had become overwhelming, with the aid of large quantities of American Lend-Lease aircraft. In 1945, General Slim launched the Fourteenth Army against Japanese forces near Rangoon, which was captured by a combined sea and parachute assault, after which Japanese resistance in Burma was effectively over. The resupply effort to the Fourteenth Army had been truly gigantic: one participant noted that 'from the spring of 1944 until May 1945, supplies dropped to the army in Burma were 609,717 tons. During the same period, bombs dropped on Germany and occupied Western Europe were 54,700 tons.'

The RAF finished the Second World War as one of the most powerful air forces in the world. Yet, with the defeat of

The North American Harvard and the De Havilland Tiger Moth were important RAF trainers of the Second World War. These Harvards were based in Canada as part of the crucial British Commonwealth Air Training Plan.

Japan, there seemed no overt threat to peace and the danger from the Soviet Union was yet to be fully realised. Thousands of personnel were demobilised across the world, although the process was necessarily a slow one. Some 90 per cent of those serving in the Far East were conscripted servicemen, and disaffection with the slow pace of demobilisation broke out for a few months in 1946. It would not be long, however, before further great challenges had to be faced.

A Gloster Meteor in Germany, April 1945. The RAF's first jet fighter, the Meteor remained in service until the late 1950s, by which time it was outclassed by rival designs.

INTO THE JET AGE (1945–90)

T HE ROYAL AIR FORCE BEGAN to be reduced soon after
the war ended in the Far East in 1945. By 1949, the
number of personnel was cut to 219,000, while bases were
closed and the number of aircraft similarly decreased. None
of this was surprising: the UK was financially exhausted and
the resulting austerity of the late 1940s meant there was little
room for military expenditure. As with the period after 1918,
the RAF continued to rely on a mixture of old and new types.
The Spitfire, Mosquito and Sunderland were among those
which continued in service, while the Gloster Meteor and
De Havilland Vampire fighters were joined in 1951 by a new
jet-powered bomber, the English Electric Canberra.

A number of organisational changes accompanied the
rapid alteration in size and role of the RAF. Not least was
the formation of the Women's Royal Air Force (WRAF) in
1949. The example set by the Women's Auxiliary Air Force
during the Second World War contributed to a decision to
give women the opportunity of a career in the RAF. The RAF
and WRAF gradually grew closer over the years, with ever
fewer distinctions being made in terms of training and rank
structure. In 1970 the first female applicants were admitted
to Cranwell, and in April 1994, the WRAF and the RAF
officially merged, allowing women to become full members
of the air force.

Another factor was National Service, in which all males
between the ages of seventeen and twenty-one were eligible

OPPOSITE:
An English
Electric
Canberra in flight
on 23 September
1958, with the
mushroom cloud
from Operation
Grapple Z Test 4
'Burgee', the
final test of the
series, in the
background.

The Women's Royal Air Force replaced the WAAF in 1949 and moved closer in role and organisation to the RAF as time progressed, before the two merged in 1994.

to spend some eighteen months serving in one of the three services, after which they were liable to be called up in the event of war. However, it became clear by the early 1960s that the increasingly complex equipment operated by the RAF was undermining the value of conscription and the last national servicemen left the RAF in 1963.

It was not long before it became apparent that British forces in Germany, the British Army of the Rhine and the Second Tactical Air Force (renamed RAF Germany in 1959) must be prepared for a potential confrontation with the Soviet Union – a possibility that came dangerously close in 1948 when the Soviets closed the road and rail links to West Berlin. In response, the US and Britain began a large-scale relief effort to keep Berlin supplied. During the 'Berlin Airlift', the RAF flew more than 65,000 sorties, delivering 394,509 tons of food, coal and other essential supplies to Berlin-Gatow. Due to the anti-corrosive treatment to their hulls, RAF Sunderlands were able to bring supplies of salt by landing on the Havel See, near to Gatow. The Soviets lifted the siege in 1949 but the result was an East–West relationship of increasing frigidity,

The Air Training Corps has done much to promote 'air-mindedness' in younger generations, as well as giving those with an interest in an RAF career a measure of elementary flying training.

confirmed by the formation of the North Atlantic Treaty Organisation (NATO) the same year.

Relations were worsened by the invasion of South Korea by the Soviet- and Chinese-backed North in 1950. Although the RAF played a small role in the conflict, Sunderlands maintained coastal patrols and army co-operation units provided observation for artillery batteries. A number of RAF pilots also served as exchange officers with the US and Australian air forces where the Meteor, the standard RAF and Australian fighter, was shown to be definitely inferior to the Soviet MiG-15. The war in Korea gave a stimulus to defence spending and the number of RAF squadrons was increased. The obsolete Meteor and Vampire continued to serve into the 1950s, but, from the middle of the decade, a second

The introduction of the Jet Provost Basic Trainer gave the RAF an all-jet training syllabus. The Hawker-Siddeley Gnat Advanced Trainer (foreground) became the first mount of the Red Arrows.

Hawker Hunters of 43 Squadron in formation. The Hunter was the standard RAF day-fighter of the late 1950s and equipped the famous 'Black Arrows' display team of 111 Squadron.

generation of fighters was introduced, the most famous and elegant of which was the Hawker Hunter. Many RAF day-fighter squadrons were equipped with a succession of different marks of Hunter during the late 1950s, and, when superseded in that role, the aircraft was given a second life as a ground-attack aircraft and fast-jet trainer.

As early as 1946, plans were made for a new force of long-range high-altitude bombers able to deliver a nuclear weapon. The result was the entry into service of three new bombers in the mid-1950s – the famous 'V-Force' of the Vickers Valiant, Handley Page Victor and Avro Vulcan. Although the financial pressure of building and maintaining the V-Force, upgrading its bases and developing and testing atomic weapons was heavy, it was deemed justified if the UK was to wield an independent nuclear deterrent.

The series of nuclear tests made in 1957 and 1958 from Christmas Island, known as Operation *Grapple*, signalled that the UK had the means to use thermonuclear weapons. A major result of the tests was the US–UK Mutual Defence Agreement, signed in 1958, in which the US and the UK agreed to share nuclear technology. Yellow Sun Mk.2 and Blue Steel, the weapons in service with the V-Force from 1961 and 1963, were in fact built with modified versions of an American warhead.

The Vickers Valiant, Avro Vulcan and Handley Page Victor pictured together. The three served not only as nuclear-capable bombers but later in a number of other roles.

The V-Force crews were kept at a high state of readiness in the knowledge that, not only would the time to become airborne be very limited but there was the possibility that little would remain on their return. Unsurprisingly, with much routine flying practice, lengthy periods on Quick Reaction Alert and relatively few possibilities of being deployed to another part of the world, there was limited enthusiasm within the RAF to serve with the V-Force.

Sir Dermot Boyle was the first Chief of the Air Staff to be a Cranwell graduate. During his tenure, he argued against the severe cuts of the Sandys Paper.

In 1957, the Conservative Minister of Defence, Duncan Sandys, produced a Defence Review. This reduced the RAF in size, recommended the merger of several British aircraft companies and cancelled a number of aircraft projects. The review also suggested that missiles, notably Surface to Air Missiles (SAMs), would eventually replace manned aircraft. The Bloodhound SAM entered service in the early 1960s in an attempt to protect the V-Bomber deterrent force, if not the UK as a whole, from a possible strike by Soviet bombers.

The development of the SAM, demonstrated by the destruction at 70,000 feet of the American U-2 high-altitude reconnaissance aircraft of Major Gary Powers over the Soviet Union, forced a decision in

The TSR.2 would have provided the UK with a world-class strike aircraft in the last decades of the Cold War had it not been cancelled in 1965.

Members of Princess Mary's Royal Air Force Nursing Service in Aden during the 1960s. The service, which received its royal prefix in 1923, has since given support to the RAF around the world.

1963 to train V-Force crews in low-altitude bombing missions. It was hoped that entry of Eastern European airspace at low level, where detection by Soviet radar would have been more difficult, may have given the V-Force crews a greater chance of reaching their targets. However, advances in Intercontinental Ballistic Missile technology meant that by the mid-1960s the value of manned nuclear bombers was lessening, and when the first British Polaris missile-equipped nuclear submarines entered service in 1969, the deterrent was passed to the Royal Navy. Although the Valiant was withdrawn due to airframe fatigue associated with low-flying, the Vulcan and Victor continued to serve for many years. Further reductions during the late 1960s resulted in the merging of Fighter and Bomber Commands to form Strike Command in 1968, with Coastal Command following in 1969.

In 1957, the British Aircraft Corporation began work on a new strike aircraft to replace the increasingly out-dated Canberra in the tactical strike role. Named TSR.2 (Tactical Strike Reconnaissance 2), the project quickly ran into difficulties. As testing proceeded, so political opposition to the project's expense mounted, and in April 1965, the newly elected Labour government cancelled the aircraft. Ironically, the order for the TSR.2 replacement, the American F-111, was subsequently withdrawn and the Blackburn Buccaneer, originally rejected by the RAF for the TSR.2, entered service in 1969.

An important role for the RAF during this period was assisting the 'withdrawal from empire'. In some respects, the operations carried out by the RAF around the world in the 1950s and 1960s were similar to those of the 1920s and 1930s, although the tenor and aims of operations in the later years were sometimes very different.

An RAF Air Sea Rescue (ASR) launch with a Westland Whirlwind helicopter. The RAF Marine Branch serviced flying boats and provided an ASR service. After the flying boats died out, ASR continued until 1986, when the launches were replaced by helicopters.

In 1956, the RAF supported the ill-starred Suez Crisis, deploying bombers and fighters to Malta and Cyprus and providing transport aircraft for the dropping of paratroops. The air campaign was short, with much of the Egyptian Air Force being destroyed on the ground. Although a military success, Operation *Musketeer* was a political failure and British, French and Israeli forces were forced to withdraw in the face of increasing international opposition.

The RAF was similarly active in the Far East, especially during the Malayan Emergency, in which the UK assisted the national government in stabilising the area prior to independence and the creation of modern-day Malaysia. The campaign against the terrorist groups infiltrating Malaya lasted from 1948 to 1959, and although airstrikes were generally ineffective, the air force's provision of photo-reconnaissance and tactical transport helicopters was much more valuable. A later but similar campaign was fought in Borneo against Indonesian insurgents crossing into Malaysia. RAF aircraft were used to deploy troops to the border with Indonesia and operations continued there until 1966.

One helicopter pilot, Mick Charles, recalled a particularly difficult casualty evacuation mission in the book *Borneo Boys*.

A Bristol Belvedere in the Far East during the 1960s. The RAF's helicopters were vital as tactical transports during the 'retreat from empire'.

A Shackleton is serviced at Gibraltar. Descended from the Avro bombers of the 1940s, the Shackleton saw long service as a maritime patrol aircraft. The Airborne Early Warning version was not retired until 1991.

A Gurkha Company sergeant major had been badly wounded but, helped by his comrades, had evaded capture by the Indonesians and was in urgent need of medical attention:

> Still pursued by the enemy, the Gurkhas were trying to cut a clearing for us…it was already getting dark and there were thunderstorms threatening all around as we set off… Although the troops had worked hard with their saws and kukris, the clearing was nowhere near large enough for us. So…we decided to lower a two-hundred-foot abseil tape, with a stretcher attached, through the trees…[The Sergeant Major was attached but] being unable to pull the stretcher up into the aircraft… we lifted straight up and, when clear of the trees, set off…with the poor Sergeant Major dangling way below.

The unfortunate sergeant major reportedly made a good recovery.

The British presence in the area was radically reduced during the late 1960s and by 1971 the Far East Air Force was disbanded, leaving only the bases at Gan in the Maldives until 1976 and Hong Kong until 1997.

Relatively brief post-war operations were necessary in Palestine, during the conflict concerning the establishment of the state of Israel. In Aden, a seemingly endless series of terrorist actions continued through the 1950s and into the next decade, in which attack aircraft made strikes against insurgents and transport aircraft ferried troops into the area. Northern Ireland was the scene for an RAF presence from the 1970s, in which helicopters assisted in operations policing the area.

The RAF Police, tasked with guarding RAF assets, was formed in 1918 and, like the RAF Regiment, has served around the world. Pictured are a 'sniffer' dog and its handler, 1973.

Decolonisation was swift and, by the late 1960s, almost complete. With the withdrawal from empire came a reorientation of UK defence, due to revised NATO defence planning which came into force at this time. While previous scenarios envisaged a Soviet invasion of Germany being countered by nuclear retaliation (the so-called 'trip-wire'), planning from the mid-1960s called for a more measured response. In this way, conventional NATO forces in Europe would mount a defence against a Soviet thrust for a number of days while US reinforcements were deployed. In the event of this strategy failing, nuclear attacks were to be considered but only as a last resort. With this change in strategy came a decision to re-orientate the RAF towards the defence of north-west Europe and the UK and to transform the air force from a strategic to a largely tactical arm. RAF assets were thus mainly divided between the home-based UK squadrons and those serving with RAF Germany. A notable result of this new strategy, which followed extensive cuts after the 1975 Defence Review, was the heavy pruning of the RAF strategic transport fleet.

The Ballistic Missile Early Warning System was established due to the threat of a nuclear strike by Soviet ballistic missiles. This image shows the system's 'golf balls' at RAF Fylingdales.

The BAC Lightning interceptor possessed impressive, if fuel-thirsty, performance. The Hawker-Siddeley Harrier 'jump jet' (foreground) was designed to operate from small improvised bases in the event of war.

The notion that the RAF should be re-orientated towards being an essentially short-range, tactical air force during the 1970s was rudely dispelled in 1982 when Argentinian forces invaded and occupied the Falklands. A British task force was rapidly assembled and despatched to recapture the islands. Although the expedition was led by the navy and army, RAF Harrier GR.3s operated alongside their Fleet Air Arm counterparts aboard HMS *Hermes*, and the transport fleet maintained a supply 'bridge' between the UK and the operating base on Ascension Island. The loss of MV *Atlantic Conveyer* and all but one of its Chinook helicopters was a major blow, and the surviving Chinook, 'Bravo November', distinguished itself while supporting the operations to retake Port Stanley.

Sir Michael Beetham was Chief of the Air Staff during the Falklands campaign and oversaw the RAF's contribution to the campaign, including the most famous RAF operations of the war, the 'Black Buck' missions by Vulcan bombers against the Argentine base and runway at Port Stanley. These bombing operations, at the

A McDonnell Douglas Phantom shadowing a Soviet Tupolev Tu-95 'Bear'. A formidable and well-proven aircraft, the American Phantom filled an important gap in the RAF front-line during the 1970s and 1980s.

time the longest in history, required a complex refuelling plan from a fleet of supporting Victor tanker aircraft, the failure of which would have spelled disaster. Although the efficacy of the bombing itself has been subject to debate, it suggested that, if necessary, the UK had the capability to strike targets in Argentina.

The gradual thawing in East–West relations during the 1980s was to culminate in the breaking up of the Soviet Bloc at the end of the decade and the reunification of Germany in 1990. By then, the last Vulcan had retired and the RAF was tactical once more, equipped with a variety of Cold War technology. Yet, as old threats subsided, new dangers would soon fill the vacuum.

The Westland Wessex served as a Search and Rescue (SAR) helicopter and in other roles for many years. This image shows a 28 Squadron Wessex over Hong Kong during the 1980s.

A NEW WORLD (1990–2018)

THE ROYAL AIR FORCE EMERGED from the Cold War with substantial forces based in the UK and Germany, equipped with a mixture of old and new aircraft. A subsequent reduction in strength followed as a result of the end of the Cold War and RAF Germany was progressively dismantled, ceasing to be a separate command in 1993.

Operation *Granby* was the name given to the British participation in the subsequent Gulf War after Iraq invaded Kuwait in 1990. The RAF attacks on Iraqi airfields by Panavia Tornados met with mixed success: the Iraqi airfields were very large targets and were difficult to put out of action, even with the JP233 airfield denial weapon. In addition, casualties were fairly high and captured aircrew endured Iraqi imprisonment until the end of the war. The experience of being shot down was recounted by Tornado pilot John Peters and navigator John Nichol in the book *Tornado Down*, in which Peters wrote:

> The Tornado was doing about 540 knots fifty feet above the desert when the missile hit…smashing the thirty-ton aircraft sideways…We had just completed our attack on the huge Ar Rumaylah airfield complex, in southwestern Iraq…I was pushing the controls frantically, the Tornado falling out of the sky, the ground ballooning up sickeningly in my windshield.

OPPOSITE: The Lightning II offers the RAF the very latest strike fighter. An aircraft of immense capability and development potential, it equips many NATO countries in the twenty-first century.

A VC-10 refuels a Panavia Tornado and two Sepecat Jaguars during Operation *Granby*. The VC-10 enjoyed a long RAF career as a transport and tanker aircraft.

Although control was regained, the Tornado's starboard wing was aflame.

Seconds later, Peters recounted:

> It wasn't just the wing: the back of the aircraft had disappeared…the aircraft was like some comet, trailing orange fire and long grey plumes of leaking jet fuel. John called up the formation leader again. 'Ejecting, ejecting,' he transmitted. No one ever received the message.

Peters and Nichol were captured and shown on television by the Iraqi forces. They were released following the end of the war.

Meanwhile, Sepecat Jaguars and Hawker-Siddeley Buccaneers were in action, the latter acting as laser designators for the guided weapons of the Tornados. In-flight refuelling was provided by VC-10s and venerable Victor tankers, while Chinook and Puma helicopters operated in battlefield support. The lines of destroyed Iraqi army vehicles were a testament to the overwhelming power of the coalition's

A Boeing Sentry accompanied by a Panavia Tornado F.3. The Sentries have given the RAF reliable service as airborne warning and control centres after the cancellation of the Nimrod Airborne Early Warning project in 1986.

air support and within days the war had ended. The RAF participated in enforcing no-fly zones in an effort to protect the Kurdish population in the north of Iraq and the Shia Muslim population in the south, in operations which lasted from 1991 until 2003.

The government's 'Options for Change' review of 1990 and 'Front Line First: The Defence Cost Study' of 1994 reduced the RAF considerably. The Phantoms, Buccaneers and Victors were all withdrawn and, with them, manpower was significantly reduced. RAF Germany was absorbed by Strike Command in 1993, and in 2007 Strike Command and Personnel and Training Command were merged together as Air Command, leaving it as the only command within the air force. The review of 1998 meant that the Fleet Air Arm and the RAF merged their Harrier units together into Joint Force Harrier, under the control of RAF Air Command; the aircraft were deployed both from land bases and the Royal Navy's Invincible-class carriers.

The older Harriers were replaced by the new Harrier II from the late 1980s, and the Tornado and Jaguar received

The Hawker-Siddeley Nimrod gave the RAF sterling service for over forty years as a Maritime Patrol aircraft. A Nimrod passes low over a Soviet warship during the Cold War.

upgrades during the 1990s. Much of the burden of the next fifteen years fell to this trio of aircraft. The crises in the former Yugoslavia and the atrocities committed there, culminating in the Kosovo War of 1998–99, forced a NATO reaction, and the RAF, with other air forces, participated in the successful breaking of Serbia's military capability.

It has not all been fighting for the RAF in recent years. In addition to enforcing no-fly zones over the Balkans and Iraq, the RAF has participated in a number of UN humanitarian relief operations. Supplies have been provided for dozens of different crises around the world, with notable efforts including Operation *Khana Cascade* in Burma in the 1970s, the Ethiopian famine of the mid-1980s and the operations of the 2000s, including the tsunami relief effort in 2004 and the missions flown in support of the UN effort to contain the Ebola crisis in 2014 and 2015. The RAF also participated in the evacuation of civilians from Libya in 2011 prior to Operation *Ellamy* and the deposing of Libyan leader Colonel Gaddafi. These have continued a long history

of humanitarian missions dating back to the evacuation from Kabul in 1928.

The wars stemming from the 11 September 2001 attacks by Al Qaeda against the United States put a strain on the UK's armed forces but the RAF met the various challenges remarkably well. Operations in southern Afghanistan, under Operation *Herrick*, necessitated frequent air strikes by Harriers and Tornados flying from Kandahar air base and the gathering of information from Canberra and Nimrod aircraft before their respective retirements in 2006 and 2010. However, the real burden of RAF operations in the region fell to its helicopters in the tactical airlift and casualty evacuation roles. The Chinook served in Iraq and in Afghanistan, where it has again, thanks to the durability of the design, continued to give reliable support. One pilot has written:

> …they are awesome beasts to fly and [have] been on continuous operations, without a break, for twenty-six years. Within the Chinook fleet there are wizened aviators

The Westland Sea King replaced the Wessex in the SAR role. The SAR Force was disbanded in 2015 and responsibility passed to Bristow helicopters, although the RAF Mountain Rescue Service continues to operate in the UK.

The Lockheed Hercules has served the RAF through a number of guises as a versatile transport aircraft since 1967. This aircraft is dropping British paratroops during an exercise.

who have been flying with the Chinooks since 1981. They…have been everywhere and done everything.

It is interesting to note that four pilots have been awarded the Distinguished Flying Cross in the famous surviving Falklands Chinook 'Bravo November': the first in the Falklands in 1982, the second in Iraq in 2003 and two more in Afghanistan, a record which highlights the age of much of the equipment of the RAF, as well as the commitment of its aircrew.

Operation *Telic*, the British contribution to the invasion of Iraq in 2003, once again involved widespread helicopter support, as well as the firepower of Tornado and Harrier aircraft. Although the invasion itself was quickly and successfully completed, resistance to the resulting occupation soon materialised. This meant on-going support in southern Iraq from the RAF's helicopters, involving troop transport, fire support and, by sad necessity, casualty evacuation, as well as the deployment of the RAF Regiment. Although the campaign attracted controversy from the outset, the RAF proved itself a vital support for the army in its operations in and around Basra. However, RAF operations in the region never really

The RAF Regiment was formed in 1942 to secure and defend RAF airfields. It has seen service around the world, most recently in Iraq and, as seen here, Afghanistan.

stopped and, the best part of a century on, RAF aircraft are still active in the Middle East. The threat to stability in the region posed by the so-called Islamic State has necessitated further RAF operations, most notably including strikes by aircraft operating from Cyprus.

The government's Strategic Defence and Security Review of 2010 spelled the end for the Harrier, which was withdrawn

A true workhorse of the RAF, the Aérospatiale Puma has been in service since 1971. It has since served as a tactical transport helicopter, supporting British operations from Northern Ireland to Afghanistan.

The Lockheed
C-17
Globemaster
restored a
long-range
strategic
transport
capability to
the RAF, which
has proved
invaluable many
times in the age
of expeditionary
warfare.

the following year, partly in order to release funds for the maintenance of the Tornado fleet. With the retirement of the Jaguar and Harrier, the Tornado became the RAF's main strike aircraft for the next ten years, and the Typhoon, originally intended as an air-superiority fighter, was upgraded to give it a greater striking capability. The Sentinel and Shadow surveillance aircraft have proved to be useful assets, as has the RC-135 'Rivet Joint', which has essentially replaced the Nimrod R.1.

The operations in Afghanistan, Iraq, Libya and Syria have seen the introduction of the Remotely Piloted Aircraft System (RPAS), more popularly known as the 'drone'. These aircraft offer very long endurance, a useful asset for obtaining information, and this extensive 'loiter time' enables them to strike fleeting targets when the opportunity arises. Although there are questions surrounding the moral aspects of 'drone warfare', the RPAS does offer commanders time to assess a military situation, including the decision on whether to order an attack. The safety of the pilot, who can be operating the aircraft many thousands of miles away, is also guaranteed.

New challenges await the RAF in the future. Of primary concern is the entry into service of the Lockheed

The Remotely Piloted Aircraft System (RPAS) has assumed greater importance in recent years, particularly in the campaigns in the Middle East. Although capable of strikes, its main value lies in intelligence-gathering.

Martin Lightning II Short Take Off and Vertical Landing aircraft (the F-35B variant) and the Royal Navy's new Queen Elizabeth-class aircraft carriers from which they will operate. Although the Lightning II programme has been dogged by questions concerning its cost and its value in future wars, there is no doubt that it offers a giant leap in terms of capability. The aircraft has a reputation for being easy to fly, and a sophisticated array of sensors give pilots an unparalleled advantage in both air-to-ground and air-to-air engagements. Coupling the Lightning II with the known capabilities of the Eurofighter Typhoon gives the RAF a comprehensive all-round offence-defence package. The replacement for the much-missed Nimrod is the Boeing Poseidon maritime patrol aircraft, as part of the 2015 Strategic Defence and Security Review. The same review recommended the purchase of the newer Protector RPAS to supplant the Reaper, confirming the increasing importance of drones in the expeditionary wars now being undertaken.

With the Cold War-derived equipment finally disappearing, the RAF can look forward to being in a relatively privileged position in its second century. Despite this, there will be many challenges ahead; the requirements of future campaigns

remain as hard to predict as ever and the RAF must continue to be as adaptable as possible. It is with this in mind that the RAF remains a small but highly professional air force, as originally envisaged by Marshal of the Royal Air Force Lord Trenchard a century ago.

The BAE Hawk has been the RAF's advanced jet trainer since the late 1970s. To many, it is best known as the aircraft of the Red Arrows, seen here celebrating their fiftieth anniversary in 2014.

FURTHER READING

Allen, Charles. *Thunder & Lightning – The RAF in the Gulf*. HMSO, 1991.

Annett, Roger. *Borneo Boys*. Pen & Sword, 2012.

Bishop, Patrick. *Bomber Boys*. Harper, 2011.

Brickhill, Paul. *The Dambusters*. Evans Brothers, 1951.

Brickhill, Paul. *The Great Escape*. Faber and Faber, 1951.

Brickhill, Paul. *Reach for the Sky*. Collins, 1954.

Brookes, Andrew. *V-Force – The History of Britain's Nuclear Deterrent*. Jane's, 1982.

Bungay, Stephen. *The Most Dangerous Enemy*. Aurum, 2001.

Duncan, Alex. *Sweating the Metal*. Hodder & Stoughton, 2011.

Flintham, Vic. *High Stakes – Britain's Air Arms in Action, 1945–1990*. Pen & Sword, 2009.

Hillary, Richard. *The Last Enemy*. Macmillan, 1942.

Nesbit, Roy Conyers. *Eyes of the RAF – A History of Photo-reconnaissance*. Allan Sutton, 1996.

Pearson, Michael. *The Burma Air Campaign, 1941–1945*. Pen & Sword, 2006.

Peters, John and John Nichol. *Tornado Down*. Michael Joseph, 1992.

Renfrew, Barry. *Wings of Empire – The Forgotten Wars of the Royal Air Force, 1919–1939*. The History Press, 2015.

Terraine, John. *The Right of the Line*. Hodder & Stoughton, 1985.

OPPOSITE
A Eurofighter Typhoon meets a Russian 'Bear'. Compare this with the earlier Phantom image. Originally designed as an air-superiority fighter, the Typhoon took on other roles as the Tornado was withdrawn from service.

PLACES TO VISIT

The Battle of Britain Bunker, Wren Avenue, Uxbridge UB10 0BE. Website: www.hillingdon.gov.uk/bunker

The Battle of Britain Memorial Flight Visitors Centre, Dogdyke Road, Coningsby LN4 4SY. Telephone: 01522 782040. Website: www.raf.mod.uk/bbmf/visitorscentre

Bentley Priory Museum, Mansion House Drive, Stanmore HA7 3FB. Telephone: 020 8950 5526. Website: www.bentleypriorymuseum.org.uk

The de Havilland Aircraft Museum, Salisbury Hall, London Colney, Hertfordshire AL2 1BU. Telephone: 01727 826400. Website: www.dehavillandmuseum.co.uk

Fleet Air Arm Museum, RNAS Yeovilton, Ilchester, Somerset BA22 8HT. Telephone: 01935 840565. Website: www.fleetairarm.com

The Helicopter Museum, Locking Moor Road, Weston-super-Mare BS24 8PP. Telephone: 01934 635227 Website: www.helicoptermuseum.co.uk

Imperial War Museum London, Lambeth Road, London SE1 6HZ. Telephone: 020 7416 5000. Website: www.iwm.org.uk/visits/iwm-london

Imperial War Museum Duxford, Duxford, Cambridgeshire CB22 4QR. Telephone: 01223 835000. Website: www.iwm.org.uk/visits/iwm-duxford

International Bomber Command Centre, Canwick Hill, Lincoln LN4 2RF. Telephone: 01778 421420. Website: www.internationalbcc.co.uk

The Museum of Army Flying, Middle Wallop, Stockbridge, Hampshire SO20 8DY. Telephone: 01264 784421. Website: www.armyflying.com

National Museum of Flight, East Fortune Airfield, East Lothian EH39 5LF. Telephone: 0300 123 6789. Website: www.nms.ac.uk/national-museum-of-flight

Royal Air Force Museum Cosford, Shifnal, Shropshire

TF11 8UP. Telephone: 01902 376 200.
Website: www.rafmuseum.org.uk/cosford
Royal Air Force Museum London, Grahame Park Way,
London NW9 5LL. Telephone: 020 8205 2266.
Website: www.rafmuseum.org.uk/london
The Shuttleworth Collection, Old Warden Aerodrome,
Biggleswade, Bedfordshire SG18 9EP. Telephone: 01767
627927. Website: www.shuttleworth.org

Central London: St Clement Danes (the Central Church of
the RAF) and various memorials, including those to Bomber
Command and the Battle of Britain, can all be found in
central London.

Operation *Plainfare* was the RAF contribution to the Berlin Airlift (see page 40). An Avro York transport aircraft is seen being unloaded at Gatow in 1949.

INDEX

Dinosaurs by

Two-Legged, Meat-Eating DINOSAURS

Ranking Their Speed, Strength, and Smarts

MARK WEAKLAND

BLACK RABBIT BOOKS

Bolt is published by Black Rabbit Books
P.O. Box 3263, Mankato, Minnesota, 56002.
www.blackrabbitbooks.com
Copyright © 2020 Black Rabbit Books

Jennifer Besel, editor; Catherine Cates,
interior designer; Grant Gould, cover designer;
Omay Ayres, photo researcher

Library of Congress Cataloging-in-Publication Data
Names: Weakland, Mark, author.
Title: Two-legged, meat-eating dinosaurs : ranking their speed, strength,
and smarts / by Mark Weakland.
Description: Mankato, Minnesota : Black Rabbit Books, [2020] | Series: Bolt.
Dinosaurs by design | Audience: Ages 8-12. | Audience: Grades 4 to 6. |
Includes bibliographical references and index.
Identifiers: LCCN 2018014549 (print) | LCCN 2018017059 (ebook) |
ISBN 9781680728323 (e-book) | ISBN 9781680728262 (library binding) |
ISBN 9781644660317 (paperback)
Subjects: LCSH: Dinosaurs—Juvenile literature. | Carnivorous
animals—Juvenile literature.
Classification: LCC QE861.5 (ebook) | LCC QE861.5 .W3544 2020 (print) |
DDC 567.912—dc23
LC record available at https://lccn.loc.gov/2018014549

Printed in the United States. 1/19

Image Credits

Alamy: Mohamad Haghani,
12; Stocktrek Images, Inc., 10–11, 20;
Universal Images Group North America
LLC / DeAgostini, 22–23; iStock: Warpaint-
cobra, 24–25 (dino); jameskuether.com: James
Kuether, 4–5, 15; Science Source: Kurt Miller/Stock-
trek Images, 18–19; Science Picture Co, Cover (dino);
Shutterstock: 90miles, 14, 22 (prints); Arcady, 28;
DM7, 1, 6 (t dino); Herschel Hoffmeyer, 3, 6 (t & b
bkgds), 24 (bkgd), 27, 31; Orla, 7; Pokpak Stock, 32;
Quick Shot, Cover (bkgd); Robert Adrian Hillman,
8–9; Warpaint, 6 (b claws), 16, 17; Zoart Studio,
29 Every effort has been made to contact copyright holders for material reproduced in this
book. Any omissions will be rectified in
subsequent printings if notice is
given to the publisher.

CONTENTS

CHAPTER 1

POWERFUL
Predators

A young dinosaur scrambles through the ferns. A hungry meat eater runs right behind it. There's a squeal and then a crunch. Now the meat eater has its evening meal.

Meat-eating dinosaurs were powerful **predators**. They could snap thick bone with their strong jaws. Some were huge. Some were small. Their large brains made them smarter than plant-eating dinosaurs with tiny brains.

POWERFUL FEATURES

strong jaws and big teeth

sharp claws

Fast and Hungry

Meat eaters' large back legs helped them run down **prey**. They used sharp claws and teeth to tear **flesh** off bones. Plant eaters would have feared them.

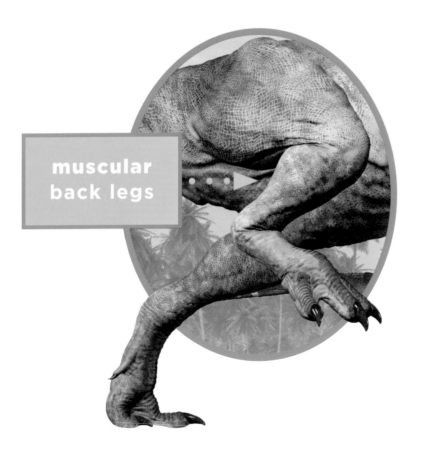

muscular back legs

WHERE SOME MEAT-EATING DINO **FOSSILS** HAVE BEEN FOUND

FRANCE
Compsognathus

WESTERN NORTH AMERICA
Tyrannosaurus rex

PORTUGAL
Compsognathus

UTAH
Utahraptor

MOROCCO
Spinosaurus

ARGENTINA
Carnotaurus
Giganotosaurus

GERMANY
Compsognathus

MONGOLIA
Velociraptor

EGYPT
Spinosaurus

9

CHAPTER 2

Compare the

Carnotaurus

(car-no-TOR-us)

This dinosaur's name means "meat-eating bull." The name fits. It is known for its two horns. This animal was fast too. Its strong legs helped it hit high speeds. Some scientists think it sprinted up to 35 miles (56 kilometers) per hour.

FEATURE FACTS

LENGTH	**23 to 30 FEET** (7 to 9 METERS)	**TOP SPEED** up to **35 MILES** (56 KM) per hour
WEIGHT	about **4,480 POUNDS** (2,032 KILOGRAMS)	

Spinosaurus could swim well.
It might have spent most of its life in water.

Spinosaurus

(spyn-uh-SOR-us)

Spinosaurus is famous for its giant sail. But that sail causes problems for scientists. They can't figure out how this dino walked.

Its huge head and jaws were long like a crocodile's. It could easily gobble down fish bigger than tiger sharks.

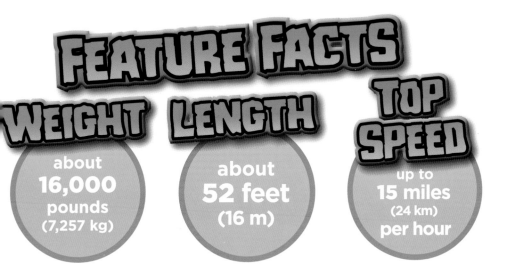

FEATURE FACTS

WEIGHT
about
16,000
pounds
(7,257 kg)

LENGTH
about
52 feet
(16 m)

TOP SPEED
up to
15 miles
(24 km)
per hour

Giganotosaurus

(gig-an-o-toe-SAW-rus)

Giganotosaurus was a **massive** meat eater. It might have been **agile** too. It had a thin, pointed tail. The tail might have helped the dino **balance** when making quick turns while running.

FEATURE FACTS

WEIGHT
about
18,000
pounds
(8,165 kg)

LENGTH
about
45 feet
(14 m)

TOP SPEED
up to
31 miles
(50 km)
per hour

TYRANNOSAURS VS. RAPTORS

Scientists divide meat eaters into groups. Two of the most famous groups are tyrannosaurs and raptors. Each group has different features.

RAPTORS

stiff tail

large hands

large claw on each foot

feathers

TYRANNOSAURS

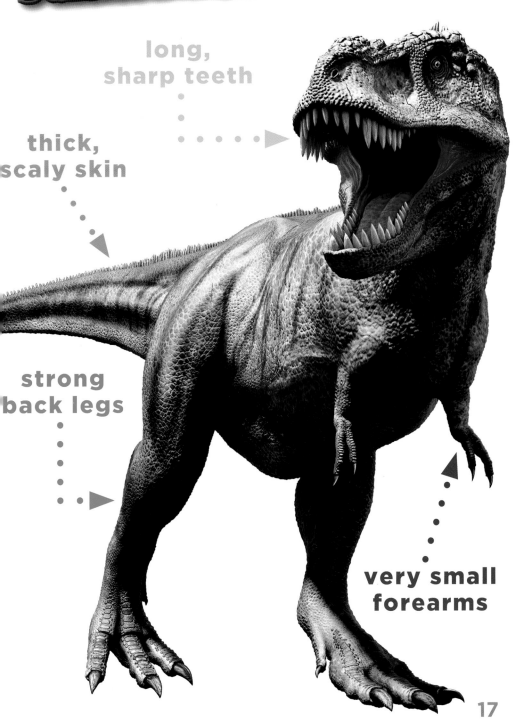

long,
sharp teeth

thick,
scaly skin

strong
back legs

very small
forearms

17

Utahraptor

(YOU-taw-rap-tor)

Utahraptor was one of the largest raptors. It was also very dangerous. Its mouth was filled with sharp teeth. The claws on its feet were about 9 inches (23 centimeters) long. Slow-moving plant eaters didn't stand a chance against this killer.

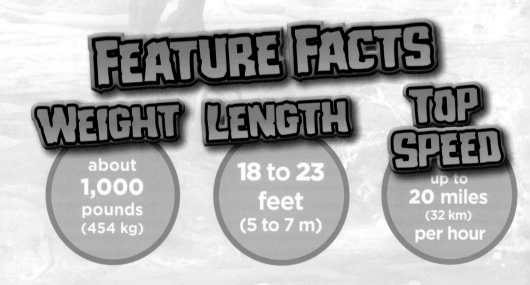

FEATURE FACTS

WEIGHT
about
1,000
pounds
(454 kg)

LENGTH
18 to 23
feet
(5 to 7 m)

TOP SPEED
up to
20 miles
(32 km)
per hour

Velociraptor

(veh-LAW-sih-rap-tur)

Velociraptor means "speedy thief." It was fast. It was also probably covered in feathers. But this dinosaur wasn't just fast and fluffy. It was also deadly. Like other raptors, it had a large, sharp claw on each foot. The claw was perfect for stabbing and slashing prey.

FEATURE FACTS

LENGTH **6 to 7 FEET** (2 M)

WEIGHT up to **33 POUNDS** (15 KG)

TOP SPEED up to **40 MILES** (64 KM) **per hour**

Compsognathus

(comp-so-NAYTH-us)

This dinosaur chased its prey through the **lagoons** of what is now Europe. It had long, skinny legs and feet. It used those features to move quickly to catch prey. But this dino was no giant. It stood only about 2 feet (.6 m) tall.

FEATURE FACTS

WEIGHT
6 to 9 pounds
(3 to 4 kg)

LENGTH
2 to 3 feet
(1 m)

TOP SPEED
up to 40 miles
(64 km)
per hour

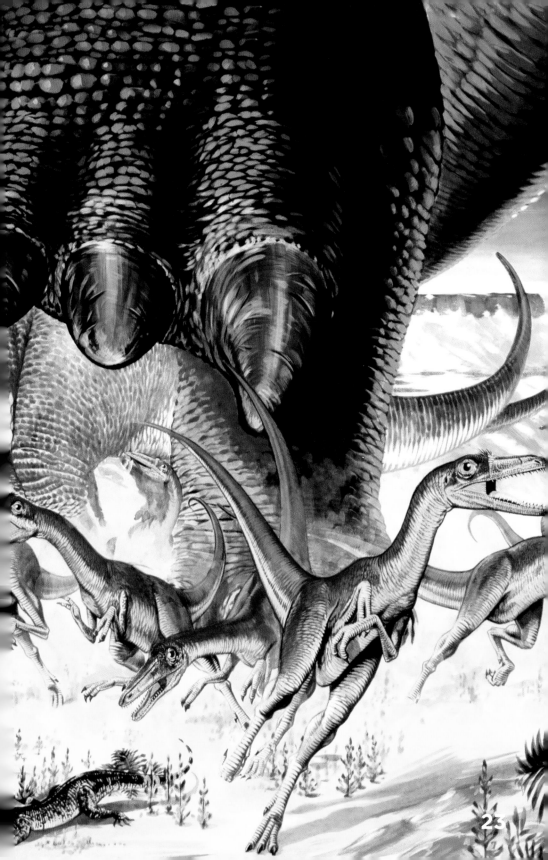

Tyrannosaurus Rex

(ti-RAN-ah-sawr-us REKS)

Tyrannosaurus rex is possibly the most famous of all dinosaurs. This giant was a living nightmare to gentle plant eaters. It moved swiftly on powerful legs. Its jaws could crush bone. And its curved teeth were up to 12 inches (30 cm) long.

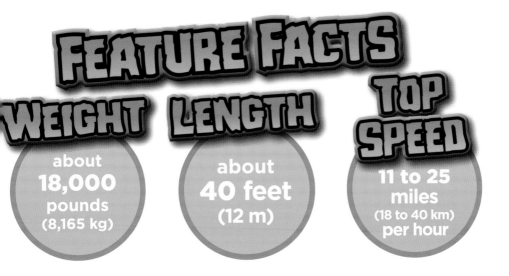

FEATURE FACTS

WEIGHT	LENGTH	TOP SPEED
about **18,000** pounds (8,165 kg)	about **40 feet** (12 m)	**11 to 25** miles (18 to 40 km) per hour

CHAPTER 3

MONSTER
Meat Eaters

They ran on two legs. They had claws like razors and teeth like knives. They were smart and fast. For millions of years, meat eaters ruled the dinosaur world. They were the most fearsome predators to ever walk on Earth.

COMPARE THEM!

Rank the dinos in this book. Then go find information on other meat-eating dinos. How do they compare?

Carnotaurus

Compsognathus — 2 to 3 feet (1 m)

Giganotosaurus

Spinosaurus

Tyrannosaurus rex

Utahraptor — 18 to 23 feet (5 to

Velociraptor — 6 to 7 feet (2 m)

FEET   0   10   2

Giganotosaurus	Tyrannosaurus rex	Spinosaurus	Carnotaurus

about
18,000 pounds
(8,165 kg)

about
18,000 pounds
(8,165 kg)

about
16,000 pounds
(7,257 kg)

about
4,480 pounds
(2,032 kg)

23 to 30 feet (7 to 9 m)

about 45 feet (14 m)

about 52 feet (16 m)

about 40 feet (12 m)

30   40   50   60

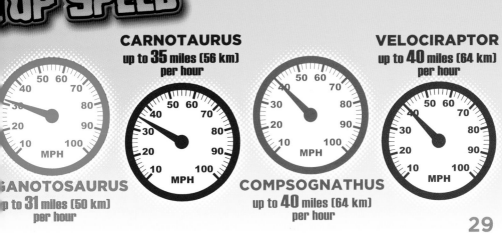

TOP SPEED

CARNOTAURUS
up to **35** miles (56 km)
per hour

VELOCIRAPTOR
up to **40** miles (64 km)
per hour

GANOTOSAURUS
up to **31** miles (50 km)
per hour

COMPSOGNATHUS
up to **40** miles (64 km)
per hour

29

agile (AJ-ahyl)—able to move quickly and easily

balance (BAH-luns)—stability produced by an even distribution of weight

flesh (FLESH)—the soft parts of the body of an animal or person

fossil (FAH-sul)—the remains or traces of plants and animals that are preserved as rock

lagoon (luh-GOON)—a shallow pond near a larger body of water

massive (MAH-siv)—impressively large

muscular (MUS-kyu-lur)—having large and strong muscles

predator (PRED-uh-tuhr)—an animal that eats other animals

prey (PRAY)—an animal hunted or killed for food

BOOKS

Braun, Eric. *Tyrannosaurus Rex vs. Rhinoceros.* Versus! Mankato, MN: Black Rabbit Books, 2018.

Grack, Rachel. *Discovering Velociraptor.* Dinosaurs. Mankato, MN: Amicus, 2019.

West, David. *Giant Meat-Eating Dinosaurs.* Prehistoric Animals. New York: Windmill Books, 2016.

WEBSITES

Dinosaurs
discoverymindblown.com/category/dinosaurs/

Large Meat-eaters
www.kidsdinos.com/large-meat-eater/

Prehistoric World
www.nationalgeographic.com/science/the-prehistoric-world/

INDEX